Published by Motiva

M000013381

Printed in the United States of America

Library of Congress Cataloging-in-Publication Data

Berman, Drew A., 1972 -
    You Online You Offline / Drew Berman
    ISBN: 978-1-935-72343-1

1st printing, September 2011
2nd printing, December 2011

Cover Design: Motivational Press
Additional Input, Layout and Editing: Seth Lefferts

"When I met Drew Berman I knew right away he was a Network Marketing RockStar. He is one of the rare ones that has Offline and Online success. Drew understands this industry inside and out, and he certainly has a pulse on where the profession of Network Marketing is going. 'You Online You Offline' will help a lot of people achieve RockStar status. Well done Drew!"

Craig Duswalt, Speaker, Author
and Creator of RockStar System For Success
www.CraigDuswalt.com

"I believe that Drew Berman understands the demand on business people, to build strong relationships with networks of people in order to create powerful masterminds that brand him as a leader, and an asset to anyone looking for answers to success. You will gain valuable wisdom from Drew. Take his advice and put it into action and you too will see massive results."

Jerry Myers, President and CEO
Freedom Now

"Drew Berman's book is unbelievable! In just a few pages he really captures the essence of the industry, the essence of what it takes to succeed. Really listen to what he has to say! Just listen to him."

David Wood, Chief Training Officer
Isagenix International

"Drew is one of the few people to successfully blend the online world with the offline world of Network Marketing, which is key to unlocking great wealth and freedom as a network marketer. A great connector, marketer, and leader, Drew will help you reach your goals and show you how the top 1% make their fortunes."

Brian Fanale, Founder and Owner
My Lead System Pro

Dedications

*For Corey, Tyler and Noah;
my love and inspiration*

*For all entrepreneurs,
seasoned professionals,
or those of you just starting
on your new journey.*

*My deepest thanks to:
Dave Schafer
Seth and Penny Lefferts
Philip Sasso
Beth Miller
Ron Reid and Luna Pang Reid
Jim and Kathy Coover
David Wood
Steve Lee
Jeff Stolper
Bill Constain*

My Roots

Fresh Meadows, Queens, NY
PS 26
Ryan Jr. HS
Stuyvesant HS
TUM
Peg Legs Football
George Washington University
Pi Kappa Alpha Fraternity
Royal Prestige
Landmark Forum
Peak Potentials
Odyssey 2000
Manhattan Apartments
Quixtar
World Wide Group
Isagenix International
Millionaire Mind Intensive
Enlightened Warrior Training Camp (AHO)
Wizard Training Camp (So Be It)
MyLeadSystemPro (MLSP)
Magnetic Sponsoring
Ridgefield, CT
Ridgefield Chamber of Commerce
NetWorkPlus

Table of Contents

Preface

The story is told of a millionaire in our profession who went to an appointment with his accountant. After reviewing the millionaire's income and profit/loss statements, the accountant was astonished.

"I need to know what business you're in," the accountant stated, desperation filling his voice. "You make more in one month than I make in a year! What is your business?"

The millionaire began to talk about the product and about the business, but the accountant stopped him in mid-thought.

"Oh yeah," he said airily. "I've been to one of those meetings before."

The millionaire was surprised. "Really? So you already know a little bit about what we do, then. What did you think?"

"Oh, I didn't believe a word of it," the accountant said, laughing.

The millionaire looked the accountant and stated simply, "I did."

We associate success with wealth. We also want to be healthy enough to enjoy the fruits of our successes.

Do you remember hearing this familiar rhyme?

"Early to bed and early to rise,
Makes a man healthy, wealthy, and wise."

As well-known and oft-repeated as it may be, this pithy proverb points to the three great desires of mankind in the 21st century: The desire for wealth, the desire for health (physical, spiritual, and emotional), and the desire to be (or at least to appear) intelligent. The order of these priorities may change based on personality, but all three boil down to one simple concept that everyone talks about, but relatively few achieve: Success!

Becoming successful in any profession requires an immovable belief in three things: the product, the process, and the presentation. I assume that you, the reader, have thoroughly researched your product, that recognized professionals in your field endorse it, and they have done so with honesty and integrity.

Due to the current economic downturn, Network Marketing as a process really needs no defense, for it too has been studied at length by many of the more recognizable professionals in the field and has stood up to the tests of integrity and replication. As you begin your journey, beware: Network Marketing can be a VERY expensive hobby, or it can be a VERY lucrative business.

Robert Kiyosaki (Rich Dad/Poor Dad), Donald Trump, T. Harv Eker (Secrets of the Millionaire Mind), Paul Zane Pilzer (God Wants You to Be Rich, The Next Millionaires), Bob Proctor (The Secret), and many other wealth and finance experts endorse this profession.

Even for those who believe they are "in a recession" there is indeed a way to RECESSION PROOF THEIR LIVES. In fact, next time someone even mentions the word "recession," how about saying this:

"What if I can show you a way to opt out of the recession?"

While some people are suffering during this economy, others are thriving. Which class do you want to enroll in? I took that concept from Jim Rohn, one of the greatest business philosophers of all time. While the news is trying to convince you of a hurting economy, you can take control of your OWN economy.

Here is another one of my favorite "pick up lines" for prospective business partners:

"You know how people complain about the recession?" (Pause) "We help them create an extra income stream to offset the current economy."

The ability to use this language with integrity and confidence is one of the many reasons that Network Marketing has grown and evolved over the last 10 years into a very sophisticated and lucrative business. Yet it is simple for someone to start, and earn while they learn. Best of all, you don't have to leave your current job or career to get started.

If your goal is to create an exit strategy, have an additional stream of income, get out of debt, fire your boss, or get rich, then Network Marketing may be for you. Why not?

It is a profession with:
    No boss,
    No employees,
    No long commutes,
    No traffic jams,
    No cost of entry barrier,
    No educational requirements,
    Little to no overhead expenses,
    Little to no risk,
    No limits to growth,
    No begging for raises,
    No need for real estate capital,
    No demographic barriers,

Huge tax advantages,
No shipping,
No inventory,
Little to no customer service,
No product development,
A supportive team that you choose and that chooses you, with teammates who share commons goals and dreams,

I could keep going, but you get the picture!

There are several pathways to help you achieve your goals within the profession that have received amazing results. Many of these tools will be expressed in the pages of this book; however, as with other tools, they only work if they are taken out of the box and used.

I can open your understanding to many of the teachings I have spent countless hours reading about, learning, mastering, and promoting, along with many of the tools that top-level executives created and used, but commitment must come from you. Come to think of it, at this moment the only thing standing between you and your dreams is…you.

My 30-second story is proof of that. Although we will discuss the power of the 30-second story in an upcoming chapter, allow me to share it with you now:

"In February 2006, I was in the advertising business when a friend came into the office and mentioned that he had lost 40 pounds by using a cleansing product he had heard about. I was never interested in weight loss as a product or as a business, but I was intrigued by the concept of cleansing. After I tried the cleansing program, my chiropractor noticed that I was adjusting much more easily than usual. When I told him about this cleansing product, he did the same program and lost 12 pounds. My father went on the program and lost 56 pounds and, as a result, he no longer struggles with the blood sugar issues he was facing before.

So then I went to work. Within ten months I replaced my working income, and within the next ten months I turned my monthly income into my weekly income. My wife, Corey, was able to leave her full-time job in corporate real estate. We love the journey to health, wellness, and the financial freedom that we are experiencing."

See what I mean? None of this would be possible except for my belief in the product, process, and presentation. The book you are now reading is a compilation of my own personal study and the concepts and applications I have spoken about in conference calls with associates and executives around the country.

David Wood, a successful executive coach and trainer, and one of my personal mentors, has stated, "students mentor students." I became successful in this business because I became a student of it and I encourage you to study the field of Network Marketing in depth for yourself. In other words, we are all students and we all help each other. We are all learning, but we have a great "learn-while-you-earn" program, or even better, an "earn-while-you-learn" program!

One could write entire books about each of the many nuggets of wisdom in this book (and again, I have already read many of them). As you read on, I would suggest that you do two things. First, envision your own definition of "success," whatever it means to you. Success means different things to different people, and it is only your definition that will motivate you.

Second, I encourage you to make notes for yourself about the tools and processes that you want to study in greater detail. The only avenue for positive change in your profession, and in life, is through personal growth. If you embrace these two suggestions than your potential is limited only by your imagination. I believe in you, more than you will ever know.

To your success!

Drew Berman

To learn more, use your tablet or smartphone's QR code reader here:

(Check the App Store to get your free reader)

www.DrewBerman.com

You Online You Offline

Chapter 1: Belief

The basis of all success begins with belief. You can't begin a new venture into the unknown without certain basic beliefs. In the Network Marketing profession these beliefs are in the Company, the Product, the Compensation Plan, your Support Team, and in yourself.

Yourself

The very first thing that you need to believe in is *yourself*. Everyone is capable of success in anything that they dream of doing, given the basic skillset that the dream requires. Not all of us can be a football quarterback, or tennis or golf pro. These dreams require the coordination, skill and stamina that come with the game. We know what we may be capable of in these endeavors. But every one of us has the capability of being successful in the Network Marketing profession! The skills for this game are easy to acquire and become a master at.

All too often we run across people who jump into the business of Network Marketing completely unprepared for what they come up against. In fact, we all start out this way, in any new business. A famous quote comes to my mind, "winners never quit, and quitters never win". That could not be any closer to the truth! Before you enter this business you should already have made a commitment, not for a few months to 'give it a try', but for at least five years.

The bestselling author Malcolm Gladwell wrote in his book "Outliers: The Story of Success" that it takes 10,000 hours to become a master of something. Let's see, 40 hours a week for 50 weeks times 5...5 years. Why not? If you believe in yourself that much it is a short time, because it is your time invested in your future, and the payoff can be astronomical. Just look at the Beatles! 10,000 hours.

Now that you have made a commitment to yourself that you are going to succeed, and that you are going to give yourself the time it takes to succeed, you need to find the right company.

The Company

Perhaps the hardest thing in this profession is finding the right company to invest your time and energy in. You have to do the research. The way that we typically hear about a Network Marketing company is through a friend or acquaintance. More often than not, we are now finding out about home-based business while browsing online, or from those pre-recorded phone calls.

Regardless of how you find out about a company, you have to understand certain things to fully believe in them. First, who told you about it? Do you trust them? It's a good place to start, but far from the place to dive in. You never know how deep that water really is until you do your own research.

Who founded the company? When? What is the mission statement? What is the profession? There are a lot of companies based on health products, cleaning products, supplements, precious metals, financial plans, the juice of a magic berry, and many, many more. Lose weight from drinking coffee? Really now! What is the mission statement? Who are the people behind it?

I can't tell you how often I have heard "well the company didn't last" or "my entire downline left in one day". Yes, there are thousands of MLM companies. Do your homework before investing your time and money.

The Product

Ah yes. The product. Will drinking a couple of cups of coffee a day that have an extra high level of caffeine and a special 'appetite suppressing' Chinese herb really be the future of the profession? It's doubtful. There are many, many companies that fall into the 'fad' category. There are better choices.

The first question to ask yourself is "would I use this, or consume this, or collect this" product myself, for

years to come? The key here is 'for years'.
Remember, five years to start. The product line has
got to match your lifestyle and belief system. It has to
match your potential customers, the people who you
will be attracting to you and your offering.

A good way to start is to make a list of all of the things
that you get really passionate about. Do you love a
clean house? Do you love the process of cleaning?
Do you love to eat right and be as healthy as you can
be? Do you want to help others get there? Do you
have a great mind for numbers and understand the
whims of the financial world? Do you want to help
others protect their wealth? Make a list of what is
important to you and then look for a company that
aligns itself with your beliefs by offering products that
you gladly would use and share with others.

The Compensation Plan

This is perhaps the most difficult area for any of us to
understand, even after joining a company and starting
to live the plan. There are so many creative
compensation plans. However, creative generally
means complex and limited. Gold and Silver Circles,
Stars, Levels and Legs; it can all be very confusing.

The way to properly investigate the compensation
plan of a company is to get on the phone with
someone who really understands it, someone who
has been living with it for years and can tell you

honestly what to expect. However, this is the exact person who will be attempting to recruit you into the company, so the honesty portion of that concept is dubious at best.

The best advice here is to find a compensation plan that is simple, easy to understand, and one that does not limit your possibilities by capping out when you are getting most successful. Many people jump companies after they have met with great success because their compensation plan has maxed out. What is the sense of staying around at that point? It can be a difficult decision when the product line fits. Don't get lured in with the belief that you can *start* with this plan, because it will be a long time before I will max out. That is not believing in yourself. Don't just dabble. 10,000 hours of dabbling is a lot more than five years.

Your Support Team

One of the things that we hear the most from people who have given the business a try, but have not been successful, is that they didn't get true support from their upline team. This probably means that they were unable to give any real support to their downline team, because we all follow the example of those who are doing better at this than we are.

Talk to your potential team. What kind of training do they plan to give to you? Is their system duplicable?

What does this really mean? In this book we will talk about the methods that we have spent years developing, weeding out the unsuccessful approaches that we were taught, but spelling out the true systems that have worked over and over again. We are your team.

Nevertheless, your upline is your resource and, hopefully, your guide to success in your company. Your downline is your personal family as such. The bigger the team, the more help comes your way. Use all of the help that you can get. It will cut your learning curve down dramatically.

Chapter 2: Choosing the Team

In the field of professional sports, there is not a more stressful position in an organization than the team's general manager. On most teams, the general manager is responsible for assembling the best team possible with the resources provided by ownership. When the team performs badly, the general manager is criticized by the fans and by his bosses. One poor decision can cost him his job. Therefore, he will carefully weigh every personnel decision to ensure success.

In many traditional business opportunities, success is largely based on how hard you are willing to work, at least in the initial stages. In Network Marketing, the key to success is in building a team of people with similar goals and passion and getting them excited not only about the product, but also about their dreams and goals.

American industrialist J. Paul Getty once remarked that he would rather have 1% of the effort of 100 people than 100% of the effort of one person. To paraphrase a Verizon Wireless commercial, "It's the network."

In fact, let's get clear with some definitions:

Network (noun): an association of individuals having a common interest, formed to provide mutual assistance, helpful information, or the like, e.g., a network of recent college graduates.

Network (verb): to cultivate people who can be helpful to one professionally, esp. in finding employment or moving to a higher position, e.g., his business lunches were taken up with networking.

Marketing (noun): the total of activities involved in the transfer of goods from the producer or seller to the consumer or buyer, including advertising, shipping, storing, and selling.

Because I am a student of the Law of Attraction, I believe we attract who we are, not necessarily who we want to be. Mahatma Gandhi once said, "Be the change you want to see in the world." So I say, be the leader, be the trainer, be the executive, whom others would want to be, and also whom others would want to follow.

One of my friends and mentors, Lenny Evans, says this: "Be the leader that leaders are looking for." In my Network Marketing company, one of our goals is to become an Executive. I teach my teams, "Before you can become an Executive – you have to be an executive."

One of the formulas I study is "be, do, have." I think some people focus on either having things or the lack of having things. They focus on what they want and what they do not have. Some people focus on the doing of things, and they do, do, do – they are in constant action. Perhaps you can picture the businessman in a suit running full speed on a treadmill.

My question is, who are you being so that what you are doing becomes effortless and what you are having becomes inevitable. In other words, are what you say, what you do and what you want all in alignment?

As I see it, there are four essential questions that you must ask when you are in the process of looking for associates (I have also included my answers. I recommend you answer them for yourself to assist you on your journey).

Who are my ideal associates?

You must visualize them in your mind and know what to look for before you start looking. When you go to a restaurant, the waitress will hand you a menu and then you will order what you want. Take the opportunity before you start prospecting to ask yourself what you want in an associate. Who are you looking for? How do you identify them when you cross paths with them?

My ideal associates are healthy and professional. They are interested in good, vibrant health and live the image of good health. They are working professionals, interested in wealth and abundance. They are open-minded, like to read, are interested in networking, and enjoy helping people. They are parents, teachers, mentors, entrepreneurs, athletes, chiropractors, networkers and network marketers.

Where are my ideal associates?

Your ideal associates are anywhere and everywhere. Now that you have identified your ideal prospects – where do you find them? They may very well be the waiter or waitress that takes your order and goes the extra mile to make your meal more enjoyable. The key is looking at people through the lens of your opportunity and seeing who is in focus. Do not confuse that with constantly "prospecting" everybody – just keep your eyes open.

I find new associates at financial seminars, BNI meetings, Chamber of Commerce meetings, my house of worship, the bank, post office, and the YMCA. They may currently be in my Rolodex. Maybe I went to high school with them. I went to college with them. They were in my fraternity. They are in my business community. They are at the supermarket and in my path when I am out and about. They are the business owners in my neighborhood and the parents at my children's school.

What makes them tick?

This is a very important question. If you do not know what they are all about, what they think about and what they want, how could you possibly help them?

This business has nothing to do with you, your compensation plan, your product or how great your executive board is. They care about WIIFM – what's in it for me? Who are you? What can you do for me? Can you solve my problems? In order to answer these questions, you must ask them, and then be open to receive the answers.

What do your prospects (let's call them new friends or potentially new associates) think about? What do they read? Where do they spend their days off? With whom do they associate? Do they want to retire their spouse? Where do they like to vacation? Are they looking for a new car? Ah yes, what makes them tick?

Here is my answer for that question:

They are well read, well spoken, and professional. They like to ski in exotic places, play golf, and read books by Robert Kioysaki, Jeffrey Combs, T. Harv Eker, and Jack Canfield.

They have goals in life. They want to let their spouse stay at home with the kids and send those kids to the best private schools and colleges. They want to pay down debts, pay off the mortgage a little faster, take that nice vacation they've been promising themselves, or make that major purchase they've been eyeing for years.

They may not know what they need to do, but they intuitively understand that what they are currently doing isn't cutting it. Or, they are already successful and want to go to the next level. Therefore, they are actively seeking an opportunity to gain financial freedom without mortgaging time with their families.

In short, they are motivated, goal-oriented people who believe strongly in self-improvement. Give them the right product and outstanding support and they will take themselves (and you) to new heights in the business.

The people I look for have 6 key skills – the ability to: recruit, enroll, train, motivate, manage and present.

What do I need to do, change or improve to attract more of them?

These four questions can help you find your mate, your job, your business opportunity, your employees, or your new business associates, but this question is vital! This is perhaps the most difficult question to answer, because it requires us to admit that we aren't perfect the way that we are.

Let's assume your compensation plan works, your product is amazing, and you love your company – the only missing ingredient, my friend, is you. As you change, you grow. As you grow, you start attracting new and different people into your life.

Most people tend to talk to their immediate demographic when they start. I recommend you seek out the most successful people you know; the ones that are already successful will be successful in this endeavor. The ones that are not yet successful will have to learn the skill sets of a successful person. Wouldn't you agree?

You need to be what you want your associates to be.

For myself, I have to be goal-oriented and driven to success. I want to win my company's recruiting contests. I need to successfully mentor my downline and share what I have learned about this business. My commitment to my team and myself requires that I continue to learn and to study. I need to be well dressed, neatly shaven, and a leader in my community. I need to do community service, help at my sons' school, and donate my time and money. I have to study from the millionaires in my profession. I have to be well read and attend leadership seminars.

Because my product line is health and wellness related, I need to be in great shape. I also need to be a great husband and father so that my personal life is gratifying and I achieve balance.

Attracting the right associates requires the commitment to be the right associate. We attract who we are.

I recommend that you stop reading right now, write down these 4 questions on piece of paper (one that you will not lose – either put it in your day planner or your ongoing success journal), and then answer them in a different color. Make sure you have all the answers on a piece of paper. Read it often – at least once in the morning and once at night. If you do this, magic will happen!

Before you continue, take an opportunity to review. What did you get out of this chapter? Do not let the simplicity of these principles fool you. I bet if you take them seriously and track your success for 90 days, you will see a drastic improvement.

Chapter 3: 8 Steps to Success

Network Marketing is a business. It is also a game. It can be fun. It can be very lucrative. Success takes certain characteristics, no matter what profession you are in. What does it take to succeed in Network Marketing? It takes dedication, commitment, focus, energy, leadership-ability, coach-ability, time management, patience, and more. We can guide you to resources to improve in all of these areas, but you have to self-assess where you are strong and where you are weak. You will also have to do this for the teams that you develop. Once you have the desire and you are ready to take massive action, then we can guide you to success.

Have you have heard the expression "sponsor up"? What does that mean? Well, you want to get good at identifying smart people who already have had some success. Chances are that they will bring their talents with them when they join your team. Can people who are not successful, who do not manage their time well, who do not have leadership skills, be successful in your business? Yes, of course, but let us ask it this way. Do you want people who are not successful, who do not manage their time well, who do not have leadership skills in your business?

Most people tend to sponsor people in their own demographic. This is very limiting. Sponsor up!

Sponsor Up! SPONSOR UP! If you drag broke and tired people, who are sick and complaining, into your business, because they need your product, and they need your compensation plan, then you will have a team of broke, tired and sick people.

That being said, you still want to see the best in people. I have a plaque on my desk that reads, "when I let go of what I am, I become what I might be", a saying by Lao Tzu. It's the same thing with your team and future teammates. Believe in who they can be, don't limit them by who they are. Speak greatness into people and you will have raving fans. Show people a glimpse of the future, give people a sneak peak into their potential and watch as miracles happen. This is an art; look at the gradient (later chapter). Don't promise people riches and fame and time freedom if they have not yet developed the skill sets needed.

When we are in alignment with what we do, what we want and what we say, magic will happen. When one is committed, providence happens. This may take weeks, or months, or years, or decades - but it is worth it. Network Marketing deserves your attention. Even if you just want to make an extra $1,000 a month. However, if you want to make big money, let's call it six figures, there is a process that we recommend. Let's just pause for a second for a mental check in. Did you read that last sentence and think six figures a year, or did you read that last sentence thinking six figures a month? Hmm, just something to think about. What kind of story are you writing for yourself? Either way, both numbers are attainable.

This business ultimately has a lot less to do with your product and your compensation plan than you think. It has to do with moving people into action. I learned 20 years ago, when I was Social Chairman of my fraternity (Pi Kappa Alpha) at George Washington University, how difficult it is to get people into motion. You would think that the main reason people join a fraternity is for the social aspect, and yet it was still challenging to get people moving. The same thing goes for Network Marketing. At first you are faced with motivating just one person to take action and make a decision. Then you get to do that over and over. So if you spend some time and focus on the process, you can have great results in Network Marketing. This process has made me a lot of money and can make you a lot of money as well.

Success is a process. Network Marketing is a process. This eight step process can help you to get the results that you wish to achieve. Each step can take seconds to learn, years to practice, and a life time to master. Any skill can be learned. Any learned skill can be mastered.

The Eight Steps Revealed

These eight steps, when learned and then, eventually, mastered, can make or break your experience in Network Marketing. Each step is a process in itself and deserves your attention. First we will list the steps, then we will go a bit deeper.

The 8 step process to 6 figures in Network Marketing:
1 Stranger to Hello
2 Hello to Are You Open
3 Are You Open to an Appointment
4 Appointment to Presentation
5 Presentation to Objections
6 Objections to Follow Up
7 Follow Up to Enrollment
8 Enrollment to Advancement

1. Stranger to Hello

Without this step we can't even begin. Ironically, it's this step that stops most people. Most people in Network Marketing don't ever sponsor even one person. That's right. They have raised their hand, they have said that they want to make money, and they can't even get out of the gate. We can do a whole weekend course on how to approach people. Whether you are making contacts offline or online, we are in a people business, and no people means no business! Step one is affectionately called prospecting. No prospecting, no business. *Know* prospecting, *know* business.

Pick a profession: carpenter, doctor, lawyer, dentist, florist, car dealer; you need people. These are people to buy your product or service and, more importantly, people for you to serve. You are in business now. You need to find customers and you need to find business partners. Some of the people you present to will be people you already know and others will be people that you don't know. Yet, which group has more people, those that you know or those you don't know?

So your first skill is to learn how to approach people you already know, also known as your warm market. Then you have to learn how to meet people when you are out and about. This is prospecting. Remember, and this is very important, you don't go out to prospect, you prospect while you are out. Then you learn how to market, online and offline, so that people come to you. When you have more leads than time, you are in a good position. As a result of step 1 you learn to develop your list.

Your List
Old-school networkers will tell you to make a list of 100 people. We say to make a list of 10. Also, don't tell your new people to go out and make a list, they

don't know how and then you may never see them again. Book appointments with your new teammates, or the new members of your community, and help them to make a list.

When I refer to the word *stranger*, I am referring to people who are a stranger to your business, who could be people whom you have never met before, who we say are on your 'cold list'. Or they could be people you may already be in contact with in some way - your warm list. Your warm list may or may not be the best set of people to approach at first. There are a lot of factors to be considered. How confident are you? Did you have good product results? Do you have a large sphere of influence? Are you somewhat introverted? Are you new to Network Marketing? Are you a seasoned veteran in a business? Do you have influence in your community? Do you have a history of being successful?

For me, I could not get anywhere with my first company, Amway, even after five years. I couldn't get results from my warm market or my cold market. In my current company, I couldn't go back to my warm market, because they were judging me from their prior experience when I last approached them, but when I started having success with people I did not know, some, and only some, of my warm market started coming around.

Stranger to Hello. This is so important. Sometimes you have to start with hello, literally. Hi. Nice day. How are things? What's new and exciting? You might be laughing at how basic this is or you might be getting sweaty palms at the mere thought of this. Either way, you will have people in your group, on your team, in your community, that don't even know how to talk to people. We can teach you what to say, but it's not the words you say, it's the music you play.

One of my friends and teammates is a musician. He showed me how to hold the guitar and twist my hand and my little pinky so that I can properly reach the strings. Even that part was painful for me. So, to really get into prospecting, list building, connecting with people online and offline, we are going to need to spend some time together to get through that difficult part. The following are some resources that I recommend.

Your first resource is at www.drewberman.com. Go there daily, if not weekly, for a wealth of professional content. Your next resource is www.YouOnlineYouOffline.com, where you will find the most cutting edge training for both online and offline marketing.

www.YouOnlineYouOffline.com

My favorite trainers on list building, prospecting, setting appointments, attitude, language, and posture are:

- MJ Durkin – known as America's Prospecting Coach and author of "Double Your Contacts". MJ teaches what to say and what not to say. To learn more about MJ Durkin, click here:

  http://tinyurl.com/3ohnn4p

Or use your QR Code Reader here:

MJ Durkin

- Mike Dillard - the father of Attraction Marketing and author of "Magnetic Sponsoring".

- Don Spini - author of bestselling "60 Seconds to YES". This is phenomenal training.

So now you have said hello, made small talk, gotten to know each other and caught up on old times. Now you transition to Are you Open.

2. Hello to Are You Open

We must find a want, need or desire before moving ahead with people. Most people will just go right into the sales mode here. Big mistake! Our advice? Stop selling! Start connecting. Sell less, connect more. We have what they want, right? Our products work, our compensation plan works. So what is the problem? It is time to find out: what is their pain and what is their pleasure?

What can your product, idea or service do for them, how can it benefit them and how can it help them in their life? If you don't know these answers then you are merely a salesman and may convert 1 in 10, if you *convince* them. This will greatly limit your success. Are they even open to hearing what you have to offer? Open, meaning are they open minded to hearing what you have to offer. Have you created a curiosity? You have to wait until they ask you for information. You can't just launch into your presentation. This is the biggest mistake that people make, and it will blow away your prospect pretty much all of the time.

Once you are asked for the presentation, are you planning to lead off with your product? Are you going to tell them how great you feel on your product that you are using and about how you are excited for them to try it too? Or are you leading with a business opportunity? I have found that while people might not be interested in the business, they may still be open to the product. It's all in the language. I do not present a business opportunity, per se (what do you think of when you hear someone start in with 'this is a great business opportunity'). Most people will think about how busy they already are, or their existing business requirements. I always present my business as an extra stream of income.

This takes a lot of practice, but when you get good at it, people will come to you having already decided 'yes'. It is time to stop chasing; stop convincing. Identify a want, need or desire in your prospect. Learn how to find out what peoples problems are and how to solve them with your offering, but don't vomit it on them. But, we are getting ahead of ourselves.

As a beginner, we tend to mush all of the steps together. We encourage you to be distinct in your communication and to know your intentions and expectations. Keep a chart of these steps and then gently guide people through the process. As a seasoned veteran, we may tend to mix the steps up.

It's kind of like playing jazz. Once you know the notes, the tune, and the harmony, you can improvise and it will sound unique; it will be your own. People will sign up with you. But if you improvise it too soon, without really knowing the steps, it will sound like noise, not music. People will not sign up with you because they will be confused. Awareness is the first step toward change.

3. Are You Open to Appointment

Ah, now this is high-level training. Step 3 can be the difference between a couple of grand a month and a couple of grand a week. We think this is where most people miss the boat; they miss the big picture. If you have gotten steps 1 and 2 down then you are well on your way. You are further along than most. You are probably taking this business seriously and you are looking to grow yours. You probably have some success under your belt and you want to have more. Most people go right from step 2 to step 4 and this is a big, huge mistake. If this step is not done right it will turn off, and turn away, a lot of people. More people will say *No* instead of *Yes* and you won't know why. Step 3 is critical. You have to make an appointment.

Remember, *you teach people how to treat you*. You do this by how you act and communicate on a regular basis. You teach your spouse how to treat you, your kids how to treat you and your prospects how to treat you. Let's not call them prospects. Let's call them new business partners, new customers, new team members or, better yet, new members of your community. You are not just building a team; you are building a community. You want to be successful, right? You want others to be successful, right? Then build a community.

To add fuel to your fire after step 2, let's practice making an appointment. Sound simple? Sound basic? Logical? Intimidating? None of the above? All of the above? Remember, you are reading this for *you*, as a student. You are also reading this to become a teacher, mentor and influencer of people. If you are at step 2 with someone and have developed interest, or curiosity, and you VV them (verbally vomit all of your product information all over them), then you are "that sales person doing another one of those things". You have lost them. You just shoved all your CDs and brochures in their face and then they said they want to think about it. Did you see their attention start to wander? Their eyes start to drift? Their polite smile? That is because you just figuratively threw up on their shoes. Would you want to do business with someone that threw up on your shoes?

You've probably been to a party, personal or professional, or some kind of networking event, and you were handed a bunch of business cards, or someone just spent 10 minutes telling you what they do. Or perhaps you are on Facebook and you see someone's profile pushing his or her super juice of the month. I know this is not you. You are a professional. You are a professional network marketer. You market a good product and/or service and you are willing to talk about it at the right time and place. Make the appointment.

Here is another scenario. Your prospect said that they would look at your info. They would review your website. You said "GREAT" because you "GOT ONE", like you just went fishing. WOO HOO, you tell your wife or your upline or, even worse, yourself. You think that you have got yourself a prospect – which then turns into a suspect. You tell them you'll call them in a couple of days, and then they join the witness protection program and won't return any of your calls. Then they end up on your never ending, 'shame-on-you', eternal list of people who are in MaybeLand, who suck all of your time and energy, and you can't figure out why they have unfriended you on Facebook. They were interested, right? Wrong!

Do you tell your doctor that you will swing by? Does your lawyer say "come to my office in a couple of days and we can follow up"? When do you go to the dentist - sometime soon? You are a professional just like all of them. You are either part-time or full-time. Either way, you are busy. You are a busy executive. They are busy as well. You don't want to get into voicemail Hell, do you? Step 3 is so important. It's so easy, and it's so lucrative. You've got their attention; they have expressed interest or curiosity and asked for more information. At least they are open. Great. Well done. "Now, when can we chat?" This question will make you a lot of money.

We should go a little deeper here. Are you setting an appointment to *sell* them your product or service, or are you meeting with them because you have identified a need, want or desire and you have a potential solution. This approach is what separates amateurs from professionals. This will help you go from good to great. Applying this philosophy will help you get from where you are to where you want to be.

How do you make appointments? By asking questions like:

- when is a good time to follow up?
- when can we spend some time together on the phone where you will not be interrupted?
- is it better to reach you in the morning or afternoon? What day? What time?

Or by telling them when you are available:

- I can speak to you on Tuesday or Thursday, which is better for you? I have 1pm or 3pm open.

After you have an appointment, confirm by an email that includes an action step.

"It was great to chat with you the other day. I look forward to continuing our conversation on Tuesday at 4pm, as we discussed. Can you be in front of a computer when I call? That will make our time together more productive. Also, will you please watch this video about how we have helped others in your situation?

If anything comes up that would require you to reschedule, can you please email me so that I can give the timeslot to someone else and prioritize another time with you in my calendar?"

Step 3 is so important!

4. Appointment to Presentation

Your presentation can be done in a number of ways. The most common ones in Network Marketing are: a video, an audio overview, a 3-way call, a webinar, a teleconference, a one-on-one meeting, a house presentation and a group or hotel presentation. Let's assume that, whether you are new to this game or you are a seasoned pro, you know how to do your company presentation. Yet, it's the language, the posture and the energy that you have in the conversation *before* the presentation, and what you do and say (and what you don't do and say) *after* the presentation, that will make you a fortune in our profession.

The presentation needs to be as short as possible. If you understand your prospective buyer's needs and wants clearly, then you know what you have to say. You should keep your presentation as short and to the point as possible. Have you ever been a witness called to the stand? Do you just ramble on and on spouting unrelated information? Hopefully not! The thing to keep in mind here is that your prospect has already said 'yes' to themselves, which is why they are willing to listen, and want to say 'yes' to you, so the only thing that you can do here is to dampen their enthusiasm with too many words. There is a quote that goes "seek not to know all of the answers, only to understand the questions". How right is that? You have two ears and one mouth, so you should be listening twice as much as you are speaking...or more!

Once you have answered their questions – your presentation – there are two very powerful follow up questions you can ask:

Question #1: After hearing the presentation, what interested you most, a product experience or the income opportunity?

For my business, my exact question is "what interested you more, better health, better wealth, or both?
"

Question #2: After reviewing our program, how would you like to see our company help you in your life?

These two questions, when asked properly, can be game changers.

5. Presentation to Objections

Very rarely do people really say 'No'. They are ready to say 'Yes' when you began. They often say no because they don't know, which can lead to objections. Let's call them questions. Questions are easier to handle then objections.

If people say no, no thanks, not interested, or any other variation, this is a good thing. On the list - off the list – no pressure. Yes or no, I've got to go, this a-train is a-movin'! Small list, big objections, big problems, big pressure = small business. Large list, fewer objections = big business. If you have a list of three people and someone has a lot of questions, you are going to spend a lot of time with this person. If you have a list of 300, you will learn how to cull out the best. If you have less than 25 people on your list, you don't have an objection problem, you have a lack of people problem. When the late, great Jim Rohn was asked where he found his people, he said, "Wherever they are".

Ironically, you will generally attract the questions (objection) that you are having the most trouble with yourself. If you think that it is hard to make money, since you didn't get in at the ground floor of the company, or whatever, that is what you will attract. If you are having trouble with the cost of your product, then people will tell you it is too expensive.

Objections and questions are part of the process. They are not saying '*no*', they are saying "I need more information before I can say yes". If they say a true no, bless them and release them. In fact, I encourage people to say no.

Here's a good example. "When we meet for our appointment (taken from the very important often neglected step 3), if I show you a potential solution and it is not a good fit, will you please be honest and tell me 'no' upfront?" (I say this while nodding my head yes...even when I am on the phone) Yes, I will tell you 'no'.

Great! Now if the objections come, you know they want to say 'yes'. Answer their questions. Get them more information. Tell them about your unconditional money back guarantee. Then say, "Have I given you enough information to at least give it a shot"? That is your leading question!

Use the tools. Show them where they can find the answer. I rarely show the compensation plan. I guide them to the compensation plan video. I rarely get into ingredients. I send them to the Doctor video or the company website.

6. Objections to Follow Up

Here is the whole section on follow up. It's simple. It's important. It's necessary. It's part of our game. You must follow up! So, here is the wisdom and the depth; the entire section. Ready? It's deep. Profound actually. Got a pen? Follow Up!! Make the calls! Call them until you have a definite *Yes* or *No*! Get them off of your list. Most people stop after one or two follow up calls. Most prospects don't enroll until the fourth or fifth follow up call. Truth!

7. Follow Up to Enrollment

They have said '*yes*'. They want to join. They are excited, eager and willing. Their credit card is actually out of the wallet. Do you know how many people actually blow it right here? Yup... they can't sell themselves out of a paper bag and they actually convince people to *not* join their company, their team, their shriveling little empire –no one wants to join. Why? Some people fear success and some fear failure. They have one extended hand, palm facing up, asking the world for all of it's blessings, but their attitude, or vibration, or energy, has the other hand as a stop sign, telling the universe 'don't trust me, don't give me money don't join my team'. Remember, most people who say yes to Network Marketing never sponsor their first person. It's all in the posture!

One great method for enrolling a new person who is ready to go is to send them an email with a sheet detailing a step-by-step process of enrolling, answering all of their questions *before* they get to these decision points during the enrollment, and then point them to the 'Sign Up and Save' button on your website, either in the email, or while you are on the phone with them. Let them do it themselves, but guide them there first.

Then, take them to the button and have them press it. You can stay on with them, but don't VV all over them now! If you teach them to do the process themselves, that is what they will teach others, without the fear of the unknown. Everyone is unsure when they are first signing up, because they don't want any hidden commitments that may be difficult to break. Reassure them and let them do their own thing.

8. Enrollment to Advancement

So, on to step 8: Enrollment to Advancement. Most people don't understand the sales process. They think the sales process ends when people say *yes* to your product or opportunity. These are shortsighted people, non-visionaries, and they will limit their own growth in Network Marketing.

When someone signs up, enrolls, or joins your growing community, this is when the sales cycle starts. The definition of sponsoring is to take responsibility for your new business partner. Help them, don't just enable them by doing things for them. Challenge them, don't alienate them. Encourage them without doing it for them. An old proverb says, "Give a man a fish, feed him for a day. Teach a man to fish, feed him for a lifetime." Get it? We go into a lot more detail on team building and leadership at www.YouOnlineYouOffline.com.

Afterthoughts

If Casey Kasem did his famous Top 8 (in this case) Countdown, I wonder what order he would come up with? Here is the list of eight steps in order of *importance*, but not the order they come in:

1) Step 1 - Stranger to Hello – you have got to talk to people. You have to, at least, begin the journey.

2) Step 3 - Are You Open to Appointment - making the appointment is the key to success.

3) Step 8 - Enrollment to Advancement - if you want to make big money, you have to learn how to advance people up the ranks and into higher pay.

4) Step 7 - Follow Up to Enrollment - you have to be professional, you have to expect greatness, you have to help people finish the deal, you must ask for the order. The way you enroll them will be the way they enroll others.

5) Step 2 - Hello to Are You Open - you have to create curiosity, develop rapport, and stop selling and convincing; focus on contributions and serving.

6) Step 6 - Objections to Follow Up - the 6th step is the 6th most important step, hey, what can I say?

7) Step 5 - Presentation to Objections - if you do the other steps properly, you are a student of the game, you have vision, commitment, leadership skills and you are in love with your company and your product, you will have less and less objections as you go down this journey. At the beginning you have to make up in numbers what you lack in skills. That will change as you and your team (and the community you are building) all grow.

8) Step 4 - Appointment to Presentation - if you can do the other seven then you should be able to do this.

If you can't call your upline, or if they are of no help, then visit me at www.drewberman.com - everyone needs a coach, and I am available.

Here is a self-assessment. On a scale of 1-10, 10 being very strong and 1 being not very strong, where do you rate yourself in each step?

1 Stranger to Hello
2 Hello to Are You Open
3 Are You Open to Appointment
4 Appointment to Presentation
5 Presentation to Objections
6 Objections to Follow Up
7 Follow Up to Enrollment
8 Enrollment to Advancement

Identify your strengths. Use them wisely. Identify your weaknesses and become a student. Learn this process. Master it. Teach it. You will grow bigger, deeper and faster then you have ever imagined.

You Online *You Offline*

Chapter 4: Stop Selling

No friends. No Business. *Know* friends. *Know* business. That's it. Period. This business is about relationships. How deep can you develop relationships? Friendships and relationships; both action words. They end in ships... ships are meant to be in motion. I'll never forget one of the old Amway tapes. That's right, tapes. I had a collection of tapes before CDs, MP3s and podcasts. I have been educating myself for a dozen years. I recommend that you do the same. In Amway, one of the goals was to "go Platinum". There was a tape I used to listen to called "Friendship before Platinum-ship"... Build the relationship before you build the business.

Stop selling. This is a big problem in our profession. Yes, you can utilize sales skills. Yes, you can be super successful without ever being exposed to sales, but this is not a business about selling. Most people sell, sell, sell. Even on Facebook. Stop that. You are not your company. You are not your product. You may make some money selling; you might be able to be successful, to a point, by selling your product. You might have a really great product that everyone wants to buy. But it's the relationships that will get you from where you are to where you want to be.

There are 5 ways to keep people loyal, to have them stick around for the long term.

1. A good product experience
2. A quick financial gain
3. Getting people exposed to a winning team, a fun environment, a community
4. Helping people achieve what they want
5. Developing a deep friendship

Three, four and five are all about relationships. When you focus on one of the five you might have someone that will stick around. If you help people with more than one then there is a good chance they will be on your team for a while. When you focus on all five, you will have fans, raving fans, for a long, long time. You will have a thriving team, a community in which people want to be involved in.

You know that you will have everything in life that you want if you help enough people get what they want. Focus on people. Focus on helping people. Yes, you can use sales skills to show people that when they use your product or service it will benefit them in some way. This is professional. No problem there. But if you use sales skills (or sales *techniques* – yuck, yuck, yuck) then you are being manipulative, which is not cool. If you promise people huge money and time freedom and you do not take them down the path, guide them down all the challenges and victories, show them by example how and what to do, then you have merely convinced them to join, and they will quit before you can even get them going. "A person convinced against their will is of that same conviction still."

Make friends. Enhance people's lives. Surround yourself with people you love, or people you are willing to grow to love. When your best friends are part of your business, and your business is part of your life, then your organization will grow bigger and faster than you could ever imagine. There are some people that you can work with, and there are some people that you have to work through. You might not connect with everyone on your team. Make sure someone does. Introduce people on your team, or people soon to join your team, to other members of your community. It takes a village to raise a child. It takes a community to develop a long lasting thriving business. That is what you want right? Why does it take a community? Because, you can't be best friends with everyone in your organization.

Upline, downline, crossline... stop using this vocabulary. How about support team, success team, partner, friend. When you say, "meet my upline" they think, "this guy makes money from me". Really? Yes, really. That is what they think. This is a big problem with 3-way calls as well. When done properly, 3-way calls can add value to your community, create a thriving business, and help you make a lot of money. When done improperly, 3-way calls can scare off your new people. The 3-way call is another form of relationship building. When you have a new team member, introduce them to someone on their support team. Help them become friends. Teach your new people to reach out to people in their "upline" to develop relationships. Its OK if the relationships begin with an umbrella of business. It is OK if they progress, because of business, into friendships. Of course, friendships cannot be forced, but they can be *nurtured*. Nurture your relationships and they will grow deep. Deep relationships will help you grow a deep business.

There are some people in my organization that I will never be friends with. There are some people on my team, folks within my community, who actually do not like me. They don't return my phone calls, they don't come to events, they don't respond to emails. That's OK. I can't be liked by everyone. On the other hand, some of my best friends on the planet are my business partners. Those relationships run deep. They run deep personally, they run deep professionally, and they run deep in the organization.

When you develop relationships 4 levels deep you are set for a huge business in Network Marketing. Potentially, you will build a business that will last forever. You sponsor Jon who sponsors Joe who sponsors Susan who sponsors Mary. You plus four levels... Jon - Joe -Susan - Mary. Four levels deep. If you are best friends with these four, you care about their family, you invite them over socially, and you nurture a relationship beyond the fact that you are business partners, then your business is solid. In most companies, regardless of compensation plan, people are linked together when they are on the same leg. If you focus on developing relationships, 4 levels deep, in each of your legs, and you teach your teammates, your community members, to do the same, then you will have a strong, balanced, profitable business. You will create a community of like-minded individuals, going strongly after the same goals, dancing to the same beat, and you will be unstoppable.

You Online *You Offline*

Chapter 5: The Power of Your 30-Second Story

You may be asking yourself, "Why should I create a 30-Second story? Why not a one-minute or five-minute presentation complete with a foolproof pitch that will convince everyone who hears it that my product works?"

To answer these questions, we should first break down the three main components of this powerful marketing tool:

It has to be YOURS
It has to be SHORT
It has to be WELL TOLD

First, it has to be your story.

On the surface, that seems obvious, but it bears mentioning, because any business you choose to devote your precious time and energy to must have earned your own authentic endorsement in your own words. Otherwise, you will not be believed. When you believe, you become believable. (Unless you are at the very beginning of using a new product or creating a new business, in which case you can borrow the successful story from one of your upline leaders or your other partners in the business.)

The world is full of examples. In a presidential election campaign, the candidate who tells (or appears to tell) his or her story in his or her own words is generally considered to be the most believable. When a person giving remarks is obviously reading them from a page or a teleprompter, it may appear disingenuous.

More than having a product or service to sell, you first have a story to tell. Your very own story, completely unique from anyone else's on the planet. We like to put it this way: "Facts tell, stories sell."

Second, it has to be short.

As you consider the message behind your story you must bear in mind that people in the 21st century have drastically shortened attention spans. To utilize the political campaign analogy, we are not so much interested in the hour-long speech as we are in the 15-or 30-second sound bite. One of the people I have studied was a Los Angeles morning-drive DJ named Joel Roberts. He is the one that taught me about sound bites. He said if you do not grab your audience in 8-15 seconds, then they are gone!

News outlets, such as CNN, Fox, and MSNBC, cater to this tendency. When the news anchors deliver top stories every hour, at best they will devote no more than five minutes of airtime to any one story. Therefore, they summarize the most important details, throw in a couple of sound bites from the location where the event has occurred, and move on to the next story.

As a society, we have been programmed to process information this way. Therefore, we should apply this principle to the story we tell about our product.

Third, it must be well told.

In order to be told well, your story must be practiced. "Wait!" You may say to yourself, "Shouldn't I just tell my story the way it comes out, in my own words, and let it be "'natural'"?

By all means, be natural and authentic. Speak from the heart. But as time goes on, you will want to practice. In sales they call the 30 -second story your "elevator pitch", because in an elevator you usually have only one chance to get your point across and it usually happens in about 30 seconds.

In the same way, you will often have only one chance to get your message across to a potential client or associate. Your story must be expressed as professionally and confidently as you can. For most of us who aren't natural-born public speakers that requires some practice. Practicing your story doesn't make it any less yours, but it will help you keep it short and well told.

Here's a step-by-step plan for organizing your own story in an understandable way. Let's use my 30-second story as an example:

Step 1: Describe what was happening before your introduction to the product. Perhaps you want to express some pain that you wanted to relieve, or some want, need or desire you were seeking.

"In February 2006, I was in the advertising business when a friend came into the office and mentioned that he had lost 40 pounds by using a cleansing product he had heard about. I was never interested in weight loss as a product or as a business, but I was intrigued by the concept of cleansing."

Step 2: Describe your introduction to the product.

"After I tried the cleansing program, my chiropractor noticed that I was adjusting much more easily than usual. When I told him about this cleansing product, he did the same program and lost 12 pounds. My father went on the program and lost 56, and as a result, he no longer struggles with the blood sugar issues he was facing before. So then I went to work.
"

Step 3: Describe what has happened since your introduction to the product. This should sound somewhat celebratory!

"Within ten months I replaced my working income, and within the next ten months I turned my monthly income into my weekly income. By the end of that year, my wife, Corey, left her full-time job in corporate real estate, and we love the journey to health, wellness, and financial freedom we are experiencing."

I've told this story hundreds of times over the last few years. It never gets old. People are interested in hearing it because it isn't a canned sales pitch. I may tailor some of the details based on the person or group of people I am talking to, but the format itself is pretty much the same.

Your story is even more valuable than mine – because it is *your* story and it deserves the same type of attention. By perfecting it you will gain the confidence and professionalism necessary to attract the type of people that will help you build your business.

Please do not read on unless you understand how powerful this is. Yes, it is simple, but it is also profound.

Remember, your product and your compensation plan work. Those are facts. Facts *tell*. Stories *sell*! You will get a lot less resistance from prospective associates when you share your story from your heart rather than when you try to convince people how great your business opportunity is.

Just remember this, you can practice a lot – and you should, but you can't say the right thing to the wrong person or the wrong thing to the right person.

Here's a tip – practice your story in front of a mirror. Make direct eye contact. You will be your toughest critic! If you can do it in front of a mirror – you can do it anywhere!

Chapter 6: Promises Worth Making and Keeping

You're in business for yourself (but not by yourself, remember, you have a team to help you!). You've taken the plunge. You've availed yourself of all the research, you have unshakeable faith in your product, you've perfected the eight step plan and the telling of your 30-second story, and now you're ready to make some serious money and help others to do the same. Before you conquer the world, consider carefully what you are going to present to your potential clients and associates and, more specifically, what you will promise them!

Most of us know "a line" when we hear it. Internet pop-up ads and spam mailboxes are full of them: Make $24,000 in 24 hours while doing nothing from home. Most thinking individuals pass over these ads because they see them for what they are: scams.

The primary way you will separate you from the scam artists, and thereby get a listening to of your product or business, is to take extreme care in what you promise. I can think of two general principles to guide you. There may be others:

1. Do not guarantee vast sums of "easy money."

Your potential clients or associates have been programmed to believe that opportunities that sound too good to be true usually are. The secret is to present an opportunity that has unlimited potential in extremely realistic terms.

Read that last sentence again carefully. The secret is to present an opportunity that has unlimited potential in extremely realistic terms. It is "the secret" because so few people do it this way.

To put it another way, even though you think your business is unbelievable and incredible, when you are sharing the opportunity make it sound believable and credible.

The sport of golf offers a perspective on this point. Many men and women play golf. The ratio of those who play golf for fun (relatively speaking) to those who play professionally is huge – maybe 100,000 to one. Obviously, not every person who plays golf is going to make a living at it.

Even though you might be a "star associate" or "executive" within your company, the hard work you have put in to attain that status is proof that not everyone else may achieve what you achieve.... and that's fine!

Of course, in an ideal world everyone in your downline would make millions of dollars and make you super-rich, but your goal is to bring people on board with your vision gradually (I'll discuss this at greater length in a future chapter). Instead of beginning the conversation with "Hey, I've got a foolproof way that we can be millionaires and retire early," why not ask simply, "Could you use an extra $500-$1000 every month?" Your prospects will be more inclined to listen to your opportunity and make a fully informed decision.

This is good language to study when handling objections. When people claim that they cannot afford your product or opportunity, you can say something like this:

"Listen, I know times are tough, but let's be honest. If I can help you make just an extra couple of hundred dollars a month, that would help a little bit, right?" (Nodding your head up and down)

As you work with your associates to build their businesses (and yours!) you will develop the type of relationship with them that will make it comfortable and appropriate to dream together about the future; bigger profits and early retirement. Prospects will always respond better to an opportunity that will meet a need, rather than fulfill an outrageous fantasy.

2. Motivators: Pain and Pleasure

From my experience, there are 2 motivators – pain and pleasure. I have found that most people are more motivated by pain. If you can solve a problem for them, they are likely to join you no matter what you are doing, selling, or promoting. If you can help them with a need, want or desire, they will go along with you. In this economy, if you can help people make an extra $200 a week – even an extra $200 a month – you would be helping a lot of people.

If you want to get rich – or at least make a lot of money in this profession – you will have to help a lot of people make some extra money. The more people you help, the more money you make. The more problems you solve for people, the more successful you will be.

Here's a tip: The answer is always in the question. When people ask, "how much money will I make?" – a good answer is "how much work are you willing to put in?", or "will you guarantee my success?" Perhaps you would respond, "Will you guarantee me your work ethic?"

Chapter 7: The Gradient

Healthy relationships are defined by successive positive interactions between two people over the course of a period of time. We tend not to share the intimate details of our lives with strangers or even casual acquaintances. At the same time, we are especially wary of those who would share these intimate details with us after meeting us for the first or second time.

Question: What's easier to walk on – a gently sloping ground or a steep hill?

The lower the slope, the easier it is to get to your destination. If the destination you want people to get to is joining your business, don't give them a mountain of information to climb.

When a business places a ramp outside of its building to assist the wheelchair bound customers, state law or local ordinance defines the ramp's maximum degree of slope. That's because if the slope – or gradient – is too steep, people who need it will not be able to use it. You want to use this same principle of gradient in presenting your opportunity and building your business.

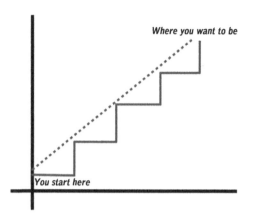

Where you want to be

You start here

Step 1: Turn everyday encounters into opportunities to share your 30-second story.

For you, as a business builder, the proper answer to "How are you?" is always "Great" or "Super" or "Fantastic" with a great big smile on your face. Sometimes when I am feeling super silly I will say, "I am amazing, but I am getting better!"

Undoubtedly, your contacts have asked the same question dozens of times and received the pat answer. They will be intrigued by an upbeat response, which will lead to the sharing of the reason you're happy – your 30-second story.

In fact, when most people say, "How are you?", they don't even wait for an answer most of the time. So how do you turn everyday acquaintances into life-long friends and potential business partners?

How about this dialogue?

> Them: How are you?
> You: I'M CELEBRATING!!
> Them: What are you celebrating?

Now you give your 30-second story!

Step 2: Maintain a comfortable ratio of what you offer and what you demand.

Remember, building your business depends on your prospect's level of interest, so consider the prospecting business as a sort of courtship. A man smitten with affection for a woman will shower her with gifts, nice dinners, and expressions of love. As the relationship matures and love begins to deepen, the man will decide to ask for the lady's hand in marriage – when the time is right. A man intuitively understands the consequences when the question of marriage is brought up too quickly.

So it is with your business opportunity. Offer value to your prospects at the commencement of your relationship. Become genuinely interested in their lives – especially if they have already have a business or a line of work they are happy in. When they become dissatisfied with their affairs, chances are they will seek you out.

A good way to practice this is with questions such as:

"How are you?"	"How are you doing?"
"How can I help you?"	"What are you looking for?"
"How long have you been at this job?"	"What do you do when you are not working?"
"What do you like most about your job?"	"What do you like least?"
*"How long have you been working here?"	*"Are you going to work here another (insert time)?"

I love this combination of questions. Most people will answer the second question with something like "not if I can help it" or "unless I win the lottery."

Then, I respond with:

"Do you keep your options open for additional streams of income?"

Step 3: To build for the long-term, find people with a long-term attitude.

There are people in the world who are looking for the easy million-dollar check. They are the people who point and click on every get-rich-quick scheme on the Internet and they are not the type of people you want to invest in.

The best network marketers understand this. If you recruit someone with a "hard sell" approach, or by promising them outrageous fame and fortune in a short period of time, they may join you, but these folks will do very little to build your business and may end up quitting within 30 days. Why? Because they joined you for the *wrong reasons*!

Too many people approach Network Marketing and forget the first part of the word – *network*. You are building a network of business associates and friends who will buy into your opportunity when the time is right *for them*. When they do join, you want them to stick with the opportunity. Otherwise, your time and effort is lost.

Look at the relationship example one more time. This is an example of too steep a gradient:

"Hi, it was fun meeting you tonight at this party. Do you want to get married and have 7 kids with me?"

Here is how it translates to Network Marketing:

"Hi, this is the best opportunity in the world and if you give me $1,000 and sign up for auto-ship and buy a ticket to the national convention and tell all your friends and family that this is the greatest product they have ever seen and you do everything I say and talk to my mentor and coach 2 or 3 times a week then you can actually get rich and financially free and you can fire your boss and travel around the world and never have to work again!!"

Now, do you at least understand what *not* to do? Remember, yes, it is unbelievable and incredible. It is also believable and credible, and I recommend that you present it that way.

Chapter 8: The Key to Follow Up

Many well-meaning people who embark on the journey to success in Network Marketing often find themselves making an unscheduled stop in a vast, uncharted wasteland. A minute spent there is a minute wasted. Several hours or days spent there can cripple a business and stunt its growth.

What is the name of this vast wasteland? MaybeLand. Once you start recruiting associates it is absolutely essential to steer your ship away from it. A well-planned follow up strategy will help.

The primary way to avoid this wasteland is to remind yourself how valuable your time is. If you were to take the yearly income of the most successful businesspeople in the world to determine how much their time was worth, you compute an hourly rate of several *thousand* dollars per hour!

Your time is no less valuable and the word "maybe" coming from a prospective associate robs you of that time. You want your prospects to give you a definite "yes" or "no." Take a moment right now and ask yourself, how much am I worth an hour? Literally.

What number did you come up with? Why? What did you base it on? Did you base it on how much you think you are worth? Did you base it on how much you would pay someone else to do what you do? Are you basing it on your pre-Network Marketing business? Are you basing it on your current level in your Network Marketing business? Or are you basing it on where you would like to be in your Network Marketing business?

Would you like to know what my number is? $1,000. That's right – a thousand bucks an hour. Would you like to know how I came up with that number? I figured I got into this business not to make $100,000 a year; I got into this business for $100,000 a month! Why? Because that's what the millionaires I have learned from have said is possible that I can make. So I took the path of the millionaire from the beginning story, rather than the mindset of the accountant.

I believe. I actually believe that I will not only be a millionaire in this profession, but I can actually make a million dollars a year in this profession. If other people can do it, than I can do it, right? If I can do it than you can do it, right?

So where does $1,000 an hour come from? Well if I make $100,000 a month, that's $25,000 a week. I think I can handle 25 hours a week of work, that's $1,000 an hour. Hmm! Now I know that might be not a lot of money to live on – especially because I live in Fairfield County – but it is a good start!

Here's how I navigate away from MaybeLand.

1. I build a relationship with my prospective associates and look for opportunities to share my 30-second story. My approach might change depending on whom I am speaking with, but the key is the same: building a relationship based on common ground or common experiences.

2. I ask one or more of the following questions:

"If I could show you a way to make an extra $500-$1000 a month, would that help you or be of interest to you?"

"How's business in this shaky economy?

"Would you look at a gold mine if it were lucrative, part time, and could fit into your schedule?"

3. Our company has an 8-minute video online. I ask them to view it and set up a phone appointment in one or two days. Setting up the appointment is key. If you are not setting appointments you are missing out on probably 75% of your follow-ups. It's so important, I want you to repeat it to yourself right now: setting up the appointment is key (remember step 3?).

Most people in our profession will meet a contact and say something like, "watch this video and let's talk in a couple of days and you can tell me what you think. " Then they will put that name and number on their eternal "never-closing-never-ending-continuous-can't-get-them-on-the-phone-leave-a-ton-of-messages-pain-in-the-butt-pretend-non-existent" follow-up list.

I will say something like this:

"It was great to meet you. You have great energy and can make a ton of money in my profession. Because you impressed me, I will give you access to some information that can help you add 20, maybe 30%, to your income. We are putting together a team that I think you will be a great asset to. Watch this video."

(This is a verbal command. Polite. No begging involved—just do it. Why? Because we have rapport, because I told you to, and because it will benefit you.)

"When is usually best to connect mornings or afternoons? Afternoon? Great."

"What's better – tomorrow or Thursday? Tomorrow?"

"Ok I have 1:15 free or I can do 3:45. 3:45? Perfect – I will call you then."

"Which is the best number to reach you at? Ok, and what is a backup number just in case?"

"OK, perfect – and give me your email so I can shoot you out that info. Cool – talk to you tomorrow at 3:45!"

Later, I will e-mail them when I am in front of my computer to confirm –same tone, similar conversation, confirmation of the video, and the time. If you don't set up definite time to speak with your prospect it then becomes almost impossible to track them down, which sets you up for a trip to MaybeLand. I like to follow through, rather than just to follow up.

4. During the initial phone appointment, I answer any questions they might have about the opportunity; usually I allow a maximum of two questions. That's right – two (2) questions. Then I will start asking the questions. I might then ask them one of the following:

"It comes with 100% money back guarantee. Have I given you enough information to just at least give it a shot?"

"After viewing the video, how do you see the product working for you? Better health, better wealth, or both?"

One of my favorite questions to ask a prospect is:

"Now that you have seen the video presentation, how would you like to see our company benefit you and help you in your life?"

Sit back, read that again, and take it in. That question – worded exactly that way – will make you a lot of money. You will do a lot less convincing and selling. They will be selling you on why you should work with them. This, my friend, is called "posture"!

Now you do not have to decide if they want the product or the business opportunity. They will tell you! The answer is always YES.

When I heard that sentence – that's right, I heard that sentence from Leann Jackson at a seminar – I knew – I *knew* – it would make me thousands of dollars. It has, and it can for you, too.

5. From that point, if your prospect is ready to join, you might set up a three-way call with your team leader or invite them to one of your company's events in the area.

Three-way calls, in my opinion, are one of the best tools in our whole profession. You get to use a product and/or business opportunity expert, for free, to explain the process and answer any questions.

Wow! When I learned to master that everything exploded. Everything.

I knew I could introduce people to other people. That is easy – let them do the talking. Done deal. Whatever your course, make sure that your prospect is confident of your support so that he or she does not become discouraged.

None of the steps I have mentioned above need to be completed in any particular order. I base these steps on the "gradient" principle I discussed earlier, as well as my own experiences in my company. However, *the key to effective follow up is following through.* Bring each of your prospects to a conclusion that removes all doubts and keeps you far away from MaybeLand.

Here are some other prospecting nuggets:

I used to say:
"On a scale from 1 to 10, 10 being you are ready to start right now, 1 being 'do not ever bring this up again', where are you?"

If they said a 6, I would ask:
"How I can help you get to an 8?"

I would never ask "how do I get you to a 10?" That would be too steep a gradient. I would then handle their objections and move forward.

Lately, I have been trying something new. Remember, I try new things as I learn them, too. I'm still a student who happens to be mentoring other students!

If they say 4, I say:
"Why so high?"

When I heard Jack Canfield say that I nearly choked. Brilliant! I have tried that lately and generally get people telling me all the things they like about me and my company and my opportunity!

When I am feeling really bold I will say:
"On a scale of yes to no, where are you?"

Ok, let's apply what we've learned here. On a separate sheet of paper, I want you to copy the staircase chart I've placed here. On the top step, I want you to write down what you want to achieve by getting involved in Network Marketing. Be specific. Don't just write down 'financial freedom'. Write down exactly what you will do once you are financially free!

On the bottom step, I want you to write the first key concept we learned for finding and keeping associates: Build Rapport.

What you write on the other steps is up to you. Use what you've learned here. Talk to your team members, your mentor and your coach. Get their input. Come up with a solid plan for achieving your dreams. Then, keep in front of your computer and look at it often. Remind yourself where you are and where you are going.

You Online *You Offline*

Chapter 9: Be the Change You Want to See

I mentioned earlier that the only person holding you back from fulfilling all of your dreams and goals is you. I want to share a thought with you:

Insanity, as defined by Albert Einstein, is doing the same actions over and over again and expecting a different result. Whether you are an executive or just starting out in your field you will come to the point where the growth of your business slows down and the "flow" seems to have stopped. When you come to these times in your career, if you continue doing what you have always done, you will go crazy. It's like beating your head against a wall and expecting it not to hurt.

If you humbly admit that you might need to improve your system or practices and seek out a different approach to your opportunity you give yourself the chance to take your business to a higher level. If you continue to be a student, your potential for success increases.

If you attract consumers, then your business will grow linearly. If you attract other networkers, your business will grow exponentially. One dedicated, experienced network marketer is worth 1,000 consumers.

Celebrate your successes where they come, but don't be afraid to push yourself and your business. Learn to stretch and add more weapons to your arsenal. There is a wealth of knowledge out there and much of it is free to anyone with an Internet connection. Use it. Study it. Make your business grow!

Take all of your skills, your talents, your faith, your commitment to self-improvement, everything that makes you who you are, and make your vision a reality!

In my opinion, your belief level needs to be high in five areas for you to win in this profession. Rate yourself 1 out of 10, 10 being absolute belief, in each of these areas. If you are less than a 10, you know what you need to work on.

I believe in my product   1 2 3 4 5 6 7 8 9 10

I believe in my company   1 2 3 4 5 6 7 8 9 10

I believe in my support team   1 2 3 4 5 6 7 8 9 10

I believe in the profession   1 2 3 4 5 6 7 8 9 10

I believe in myself   1 2 3 4 5 6 7 8 9 10

I believe in you, more than you will ever know.

Chapter 10: You Online/You Offline

Our business is going through a significant shift. Shift happens! We all need to be ahead of the curve. In order to thrive in our business, we need to understand the past, present and future of Network Marketing. The profession of Network Marketing has matured through the years and it is now ready for the biggest breakthrough in its history.

The past is past, we can learn from it of course, but we always need to be grounded in the basics. The basics of Network Marketing are simply P-P-P; people + product = profit. It's the same with any profession. Same with Nike. Same with AT&T. Same with Pepsi. Network Marketing is about serving people with an amazing line of products, while generating income for ourselves and our families. The more people that buy into our product line, the more income for us. That's it. Period.

The present state of our profession is somewhat confusing and a bit uncertain. Where does the Internet fit in exactly? What game are you playing? Are you a network marketer learning to market online? Are you an Internet marketer trying to learn the basics of Network Marketing? There is a lot to talk about and to evaluate. Some of you have no interest in online activities and have no idea what marketing is. Some of your teammates think that *they are* the company, they are the product, and their Facebook picture (their Facebook avatar) is a picture of their super juice of the month. Wrong!

When building an online and offline business, and when striving to combine the two, we have to address who *you are*, and who *you are being*, both online and offline. Your company will certainly

have a way that they market, with some restrictions on what you can do online. Some of your teammates are only using their corporate replicated website (yourname.company.com).

However, things are changing and they are changing fast. For many years people will continue to market the traditional way, or showcase their products or opportunity this way. There is a big difference when moving online. One needs to understand the essence of marketing to be successful at both. What it means to showcase your product or opportunity in a way that attracts people to you; people who already have a need for your product, idea or service. For instance, Facebook is a social platform; you should have pictures of your family, your kids, you doing fun stuff. It's not the place to always be selling.

The future of our profession is changing dramatically. The Internet is still very new (less than 15 years old!) and yet Facebook is here to stay. Personal branding is key. This concept will get more and more important as the years go by. People will want to know all about you, why they should join up with you, and how you can help them. There will always be some people who lead with their product and there will always be some who lead with the opportunity. There will be many who fail, but there will be many more who succeed now, thanks to branding online.

Fortunes are going to be made, online and offline, in the next few years. There is an unprecedented wave of change coming our way. I am sure that you have heard this before: there are three types of people; those who make things happen, those who watch things happen, and those who wonder, "Hey, what happened?" Which group do you want to be in?

I can't possibly teach you all there is to know about being online in this book. Things are changing daily. If I told you everything that I know it would bore some of you and excite others. I can rattle off the importance of having a blog, having a presence on Facebook, the difference between a group page and a fan page, how to generate leads on Linkedin, what the best pay strategies are and the best free strategies, or what are the best keywords and how to find them. Then there is how to use your corporate site and what other systems are out there to use and how. What a Squidoo 'lens' is and how to use HootSuite, PPC vs PPV and when to market what, and what to market when. Everything I know and use, learned through trial and error, is at www.YouOnlineYouOffline.com. Join me there.

You now have wings, my friend. The roots of Network Marketing run deep and this profession is *the* one to watch. We are attracting athletes, doctors, stay-at-home moms, millionaires, real estate agents, authors, speakers, 20-somethings and baby boomers. Some of you prefer to pick up the phone and call people while others like to meet belly-to-belly. If you don't show some of your teammates, current and future, how to tweet and post for profit they will never become successful.

For those of you who do not know what Google+ is, or how to use Google Analytics, or what the heck Market Samurai is, don't worry. You can't learn it all in a day, and you may never catch up with all of it, which is OK as well. I recommend the Learn and Earn program. Keep learning, keep earning! This is the key to this whole book. This point is going to be relevant and timely for the immediate future of Network Marketing and, in my opinion, will separate the people who do well and those who do great. Those who catch the wave and learn how to market themselves online *and* offline are the ones who will make it big.

For those of you who stay offline, old school, the times they are a-changin'! It's time to plug in, understand when and what to tweet, and when and how to automate things online. Learn how to generate online leads. For the online marketers out there, the 20-somethings out of school who have never used a payphone, and the experts on data capture pages who have lead generation systems out the wazoo, but get nauseous with the thought of building a business by actually being *on the phone with people* - YUCK...just shoot me! I think you are in for a rude awakening.

www.YouOnlineYouOffline.com is the way of the future, my friend. The essence of who are you *being*. Who are you? Once you are clear about this and your message stays consistent, whether at a Chamber of Commerce event, or when you are connecting with someone on Plaxo, you will be most successful. You want to be *you*; brand yourself, not your company. Make connections with real people, whether it be at a BNI morning breakfast opportunity meeting, or when you are connecting with someone from your DISCUS account.

The network marketers who are going to create long-term, passive and residual income, are the ones who have more leads than they have time for. They have learned how to talk to their warm market, how to meet people when they are out and about, and then how to turn them into leads, in that order. The ones who can do that, and teach it, are the ones who are going to win, and win big in Network Marketing.

So, I leave you with this. Congratulations on your Commencement.   The college graduation, the ending of school, the commencement, is the beginning of life and pursuit of a career. The end of this book brings the beginning of your learning. We are committed to bringing the best of the best of online and offline marketing techniques, what's working now, and future predictions at www.YouOnlineYouOffline.com.

The Internet is the new frontier, but don't get lost in cyberspace, you still have to pick up the phone. The easiest place to start online with minimal barriers, even for the technophobes, is Facebook. Once you have an account, make some friends; join some groups, just like you would offline. Then look into a fan page and maybe form a group. A good stepped goal is to connect with 50 friends, then 500 friends, then 5000 friends. Post interesting thoughts that express who you are. Eventually, you might look into a Pay-Per-Click (PPC) campaign.

(Bonus hint: the best course I have ever seen on Facebook is www.secret2fb.com).

Stay excited, stay committed, stay informed, stay in the game! It is your future we are talking about and you now have great tools to take you to new heights in your business - online and offline. See you up there!

www.YouOnlineYouOffline.com

If you found this book to be valuable, please refer your teams to www.YouOnlineYouOffline.com. There you will find constant updates and cutting edge material on the Network Marketing community.

Stay tuned for audio training, workbooks, DVD training, one-on-one and group coaching, and other great tools to help you reach your goals in Network Marketing.

I am currently available for one-on-one and group coaching. For one on one coaching, sessions are $200 an hour. Eight sessions can be purchased in advance for $1,000. For group coaching, 10 person minimum, 4 sessions are $297 per person. These calls will get you and your team coal iron HOT.

I can be contacted about one-on-one and group coaching at www.drewberman.com

www.DrewBerman.com

You Online *You Offline*

A Call To Action!

If you would like the most powerful and proven 7-step marketing blueprint that will unleash a flood of traffic to your website and create cash on demand globally, even while you sleep, then use your QR code reader here:

You Online *You Offline*

Drew's Words of Wisdom

So, who am I? I am www.drewberman.com. I have been in sales and marketing for more than 20 years, and Network Marketing for over 10 years. I was introduced to Network Marketing in 2001 when I was 29 years old, after I came back from a bicycle ride around the world. I completed the 35-Country Bike Tour and I was trying to get back into real estate.

I attended a BNI meeting and I met a man there who introduced me to the Network Marketing profession. He started by developing a rapport, he was creating a relationship, and then he complimented me. He said, "you seemed like a sharp guy. Are you locked into what you're doing or you're open-minded for other streams of income?" He gave me a CD called 'High Tech and High Touch'. The next thing I knew, I was in Amway. I had no idea, because they were re-branding as Quixtar.

So, for five years I chased the dream and the sizzle, but I could never find the steak. I can't say anything bad about the Amway Corporation. They've done great things for this profession. They do billions of dollars in sales a year around the globe. So do the other major NM companies - The Big 5 I call them: Amway, Avon, NuSkin, HerbaLife and Mary Kay. These are, or were, the giants of the industry.

However, the Baby Boomers remember what it was like when people had garages full of the soap and shampoo and they are reluctant to join this profession. Now, the twenty-somethings are entering the workforce with no history and with no pre-conceived notion of this profession.

So how do you talk to both groups? How do you offer Network Marketing to professionals who are used to having a boss, but who are entrepreneurial? Well, this is no secret sauce.

This is why we have created our new website called www.YouOnlineYouOffline.com. *Who are you*? Not so much of *what* are you doing, but *who* are you being. You attract who you are, not who you want to be. Please visit it now to change your future!

If you look on drewberman.com you can see some of the people that I have hung out with. You will see Cynthia Kersey, who wrote the book 'Unstoppable'. There is a picture of me with Jack Canfield, from the bestselling Chicken Soup series. There is also a picture of me with Deepak Chopra!

So, here is a tip for you when you're out about, whenever you are at events or functions with anyone credible, just get your picture taken with them. This is essential for personal branding. When you get your picture taken with experts, people then assume htat you are an expert.

There is a picture of me with Jeffrey Combs. We did two training programs together last year. We shared the stage together and it was awesome. There is a picture of me with Dr. John Gray from "Men are From Mars and Women are from Venus".

John Gray, Jack Canfield and I all work in the same profession and in the same company. We are trainers for a company that is the world leader in nutritional cleansing. We promote an anti-aging and fat-burning system that rids the body of toxins and impurities, releasing excess weight in the process. John Gray lost nearly 30 pounds with the products. He began to see brain chemistry shifting, with women increasing levels of serotonin and men of dopamine. After seeing this incredible change in people, he became a national trainer. So did I.

You will also see me with Les Brown (perhaps the most popular motivational speaker alive today) and Harv Eker (from Millionaire Mind Intensive). Does this make me great or better? No. What it does mean is that I carry my camera with me when I'm out and about. I know how to connect with folks and that is a wonderful asset.

Here is a good question: how do make someone appear in you life? You make them a PEER in your life. Then people will come to you. You look at people online with all of these marketing systems and blogs and they are just regular people. So, when you meet them, go say, "Hi". Get your picture taken with them, because that's how people are going to remember you, and that's how you'll create a list of professionals and experts.

So, brand yourself, because you are not your company, you are not your product. You are you, and *who you are* is going to change everything for you.

Ten years in Network Marketing and five years in Amway. I couldn't make it work. I really couldn't turn it into income. Here is another lesson, don't quit. The profession works.

You just have to find the right vehicle, the right team, and the right timing.

Go for it! Become a rockstar!

CPSIA information can be obtained at www.ICGtesting.com
Printed in the USA
LVOW012110100413

328571LV00022B/685/P